WHEN JAMESTOWN WAS A COLONIAL CAPITOL

in 1620, the wharves were filled with fragrant tobacco, the blacksmith's shop rang with the sound of his hammer, and copper-colored Indians walked among the colonists, carrying furs to trade in the market.

The exciting story of George Hall, a ten-year-old drummer boy, is based on firsthand source material. It recreates the daily life of the colonists in times of peace and prosperity as well as during the terrifying Indian massacres of 1622.

Old prints, engravings, and color illustrations enrich the text and lend authenticity to the dramatic account of the Virginia colony that planted the seeds of colonial independence that later grew into the American Revolution.

How They Lived books have been carefully developed by Garrard to give greater meaning to the study of American history. Young readers will develop a deeper understanding and appreciation of the beginnings of our nation as they see life in the past through the eyes of the people who lived it.

When Jamestown Was A Colonial Capital

When
Jamestown Was
A Colonial Capital

BY MARY EVANS ANDREWS

ILLUSTRATED BY RUSSELL HOOVER

GARRARD PUBLISHING COMPANY
CHAMPAIGN, ILLINOIS

To my brother, Frank W. Evans, Jr.,
in memory of our happy childhood
visits to Jamestown Island

Picture credits:

Colonial National Historical Park, Jamestown, Virginia: p. 18, 72
Colonial Williamsburg, Williamsburg, Virginia: p. 50, 63
Culver Pictures: p. 16, 49, 71, 81
Folger Shakespeare Library: p. 36
Historical Pictures Service: p. 2–3, 6, 33, 85, 88, back cover spot
Picture Collection, New York Public Library: p. 5
Rare Book Division, New York Public Library: p. 11, 57, 78, 79
Smithsonian Institution: p. 39, 40, 41
Virginia State Library: p. 31

Endsheets: *The Marketplace at Jamestown, 1619* by Sidney King.
Courtesy of Colonial National Historical Park, Jamestown, Virginia

Contents

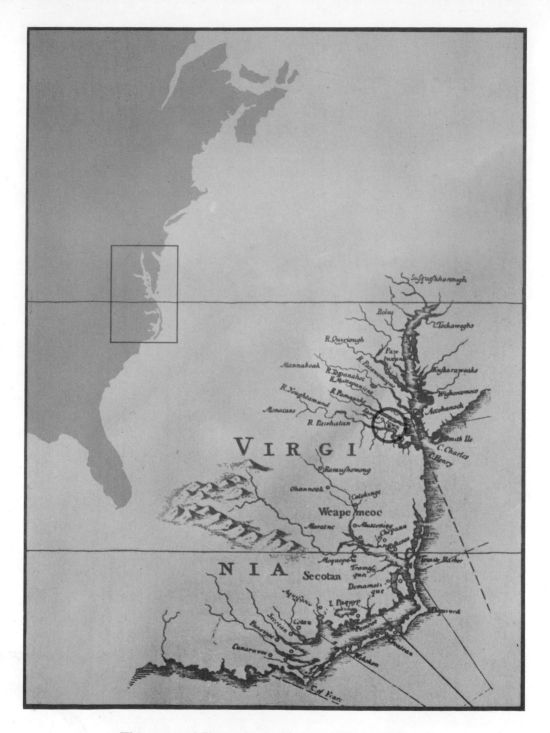

This map of Virginia, drafted in 1630, included the eastern part of present-day North Carolina. James Citty, within the circle, stood on the banks of the Powhatan, or James River.

1. James Citty—At Last

A huge wave crashed over the bow of the sailing vessel *Supply*. Bound from England to Virginia in the winter of 1620, she was battling a furious Atlantic storm. Every timber of her 70 tons creaked with the struggle.

George Hall, a ten-year-old drummer boy, gripped the edge of his bunk in the crowded forward cabin. His taller teen-age bunkmate, Thomas Tracy, braced himself with his feet to keep from rolling out.

Tom's father, William Tracy, had charge of this shipload of 50 colonists. Carrying everything they would need, from nails to millstones, they were going to build a better life for themselves in Berkeley. This was a new outpost of Jamestown, first permanent English settlement in North America.

Another giant wave slammed into the *Supply*. George's drum, jolted from the wall peg beside his bunk, banged across the cabin floor.

As he jumped up to catch it, George was flung violently against a post. Pain shot down his left arm.

"Tom," he yelled, "grab my drum 'fore it gets stove in!"

Tom's head bumped the low ceiling of the cabin, but he recovered the drum. Then he helped George back to their bunk.

George clutched his left elbow. "My arm's broken," he groaned.

"I'm sorry, laddie," said the woman in the next bunk, holding her sobbing child. Others in the cabin were seasick.

"Lie still, now" Tom told George. "I'll fetch Chaplain Pawlet." The chaplain, who was also the ship's doctor, set George's arm in wooden splints and bound it with strips of cloth. He had no medicine to ease the pain.

George lay back on his lumpy, straw-filled pad and pulled up his one rough blanket. He

was afraid the arm might make him feverish. Doctors in those days tried to cure fever by letting blood out of a small vein. George dreaded such a cure.

Tom brought him water in a wooden mug. Though it tasted of the barrel where it had been stored for weeks, he drank it all. But he could not face dinner—the usual gray stew of dried peas in which floated lumps of greasy salt pork.

Toward morning the sea grew calmer. George ate breakfast with the other passengers at a long narrow table. It was bolted to the floor in the center of the cabin. As a special treat he was given "gentlemen's food"—raisins in his thin oatmeal and cheese with his hardtack, which was ship's bread.

The real treat was climbing up on deck to breathe the clean salt air. In the seventeenth century people thought bathing unhealthy, so the crowded cabin was stuffy and smelly.

When the sun had dried the deck, the passengers spread their bedding outside and scrubbed the cabin with sea water and vinegar. They were bone-weary of shipboard life.

Since leaving England on September 18, 1620, the *Supply* had been a hard-luck ship.

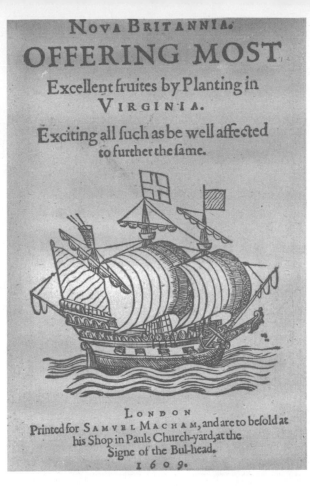

In 1609, colorful posters urged Englishmen to settle in the colony of Virginia.

First she had sprung a leak and limped back to an Irish port for repairs. On the high seas again, she had to watch out for Spanish ships, since England and Spain were enemies. Now this storm had driven the *Supply* far off her safe course.

During the dangerous days after the gale, George dreamed of what lay ahead. He had promised to work seven years to repay the

Virginia Company of London for his fare. The Company, a group of businessmen who had started the colony in Virginia, would then give him land of his own—50 acres of it.

In England, with its class system, he could never have owned land. But in this wonderful new country he could become a landowner. He would plant tobacco. With farm tools and seed provided by the Company and with his own hard work, he might become rich!

A month after the storm, the captain said they were near the Virginia Capes. On January 29, 1621, George heard the lookout's happy shout, "Land, ho!"

The passengers pushed out on deck. Men clambered up into the rigging and cheered. George gazed at the tawny sand banks of Cape Henry and the wide waters of Chesapeake Bay.

Several hours later the *Supply* rounded Point Comfort and dropped anchor in Hampton Creek. George was thrilled to see the English flag floating over twin log forts, one on each side of the creek. Before the little settlement, called Elizabeth Citty, lay the broad harbor of Hampton Roads. Behind it stood forests of splendid trees.

The new land was very different from home. At Bristol, England, stone buildings rose on the sides of steep hills. Here the land lay as flat as a table top, but how rich and inviting it looked to the sea-weary voyagers.

Elizabeth Citty folk gave them a hearty welcome. Several Indians watched silently. George stared at them, for the copper-hued Americans were so handsome, tall, and still.

Old settlers led the new arrivals into one of the forts where great fires warmed the rooms. While they held a service to thank God for their safe journey, food was prepared for them. For the first time in months, they drank fresh water. And they feasted on roasted oysters, venison (deer meat), Indian beans, corn bread, and boiled pumpkin.

The newcomers rested for several days at the fort. Then they sailed out into Hampton Roads and up the broad James River.

Now they had their first good look at the country. To the English city dweller, "country" meant neatly hedged farm fields. They gazed in wonder at the rich, wild beauty of Virginia. The oaks and pines were the largest they had ever seen. Wedges of wild ducks flew above the marshes. Once or twice the ship passed

14

Indians in log canoes. But the endless forest appeared almost empty of people. The small English settlements were few and far between.

Some 30 miles upriver the *Supply* rounded a long point, and the travelers had their first glimpse of "James Citty," capital of Virginia. The village, later to be called Jamestown, did not look much like a city. George could see only two streets of straggling frame houses and a three-sided log fort that appeared to be abandoned.

As the *Supply* tied up at the wharf, a small crowd gathered. Governor Sir George Yeardley and several other leaders welcomed the new colonists. George noticed that the Governor had a military escort but no drummer.

The *Supply* had barrels of badly needed salt and other cargo for the capital. Then she would go on to Berkeley, some 20 miles upriver.

Chaplain Pawlet and the Tracys were invited to spend the night at the Governor's house. George and the others stayed aboard ship. Watching a winter sunset redden the broad river, they talked of the work they would do at Berkeley. Listening to them, George wondered, "What work will I be able to do with one arm in a sling?"

2. A Tour of James Citty

A crowing cock in James Citty awakened George. On this bright winter morning the new colonists were to be shown around the town. Soon his boots were pounding the planks of the short wharf as he hurried ashore with the others.

At the foot of the dock, George saw a long shed. Inside, dried tobacco in barrels awaited shipment to England. Its fragrance mingled with the scent of pines and wood smoke in the frosty air.

Gathering the group around him, the guide explained the lay of the land. James Citty stood on a peninsula that was almost an island, 3 miles long and from 300 to 2,000 yards wide. It lay parallel to the nearby north bank of James River. The peninsula was shaped like a broad leaf attached to the mainland by a narrow stem of land, or isthmus. Back River, a marshy branch of the James, separated the peninsula from the mainland. During storms the two rivers would meet and cover the stem of land. But most of the time people could cross the isthmus to the mainland along the Great Road.

Half the peninsula combined splendid forests and little meadows; half was marshland. In some places narrow ridges of high ground were separated by wide avenues of marsh.

To his left George saw the overgrown ruins of James Fort, where the first James Citty had stood.

"We outgrew the fort," the guide told them. "Now the Indians are peaceful, so we've no need to live behind walls."

"What if the Spaniards come?" someone asked.

"Let them! We have cannon mounted along

the waterfront and in the blockhouses. There's one blockhouse yonder at the isthmus, the only land approach to town. The other blockhouse stands at the point where Back River is narrowest."

The group walked a short way along the waterfront to a large storehouse. The store-keeper showed them iron hardware, bottles, bronze thimbles, needles, pewter spoons, and crockery, all from England. The colonists were not yet able to make these things for them-

1. James River 3. The Peninsula 5. Great Road
2. Back River   4. James Fort   6. Blockhouse

selves. George was startled to see that everything was priced at so much tobacco instead of money.

Farther down the shore a fishing boat had just landed. Two men were loading a cart with baskets of mackerel, perch, and winter shad. They tossed the smallest fish to several grunting pigs. Pigs were the garbage collectors of James Citty. Trash that they could not eat had to be buried in deep holes.

The guide led the group along the frozen rutted cart track past the blacksmith's shop. George heard the roar of a forge and the clang of a hammer. The smith was mending tools, the guide told them.

Nearby stood the church with pine woods behind it. Then there was the marketplace, where townsfolk and Indians came to trade. At one of the crude stalls, three tall Indians were standing.

They wore deerskin cloaks and moccasins. Each had shaved the hair on the right side of his head to keep it from becoming tangled in his bowstring. On the left side the long hair was braided over the man's shoulder. On top of each warrior's head, a crest of hair stood up like a cock's comb.

George edged closer to watch. The Indians were offering to trade furs, handwoven baskets, and fresh-killed turkeys. A village merchant showed them small knives, scissors, tin mirrors, and strings of bright-colored beads.

The group then walked east, where most of the houses stood, along the River Highway and the Back Street. This was the New Town.

A few homes were one-room cottages built in the old style of "wattle and daub." The walls were made of upright poles between

which was a basketwork of woven twigs, or wattle. This was coated inside and out with daub, wet clay mixed with straw. George touched the daub; it felt hard as brick.

Old-style chimneys were built of oblong clay loaves called "cats," stacked inside a framework of saplings. The windows had solid wood shutters. Most houses were roofed with bark shingles; one or two were thatched with reeds.

A spark from the chimney could easily set such roofs afire.

The newer homes stood on brick foundations and had brick chimneys. All were modest frame houses of one or two stories with an attic above. Each had a large garden, fenced to keep out the pigs.

In one yard George saw a slender black-haired boy chopping wood. He wore English clothes, but his skin had a coppery tint. "An Indian lad," the guide said. "The people who live there are raising him as a Christian."

A large double house on the Back Street was Governor Yeardley's home. The Governor's Council of eight men met here.

Not far away stood James Citty's largest building, the new warehouse. It held goods awaiting export to England and supplies such as corn and salt fish which belonged to the Virginia Company of London. Workmen rolled barrels marked "SALT" into the warehouse. One man had brown skin and tightly curling black hair. George had never seen anyone like him.

"He's a Negro," the guide explained. "About twenty Negroes were brought here in 1619 by a Dutch warship from the West Indies. They're working their seven years for the Company, same as the rest of us. Most of them live at the Governor's big farm farther up the James."

The guide pointed off to the north where smoke was rising. "Yonder's the Pitch and Tar Swamp," he said. "They burn wood there to make tar, charcoal, and potash."

The brook called Orchard Run formed the eastern limit of the town. Farm homes were scattered over the island.

The group returned to the ship for a lunch of corn bread and broiled fresh fish. Then George was summoned to the captain's cabin. There sat Mr. Tracy with a smiling younger man.

"George," said Mr. Tracy, "it seems best for you to stay here in James Citty until your arm has mended. This is Mr. William Spencer. You will live with him and his good wife. Help them as much as you can. Go and bring your things."

George hated to leave his friends, but he had to obey.

"Godspeed unto you, lad," Mr. Tracy added kindly.

"Thank you and Godspeed unto you too, sir," George answered. He hoped his arm would mend quickly.

3. Strange New Home

George strode along the river road beside Mr. Spencer. His drum was slung over his back; his good hand gripped his bundle of clothes. Mr. Spencer carried a gift from Mr. Tracy, a sack of salt.

Everyone they met knew William Spencer. He had come to James City in 1607. Captain John Smith, a leader of the first colonists, had called him "honest and valiant." In 1614 he was among the first men freed from service to the Company and given land.

William Spencer's land was downriver toward the Goose Hill Marshes. As the two approached the house, a boy about seven years old dashed out.

"Will," said his father, "I've brought you a playfellow. This is George Hall."

Mistress Spencer appeared in the doorway. George set down his bundle and made her his best bow.

She smiled at him. "Come in, George, and welcome. Will, take his bundle and show him to the loft."

George followed Will up the steep ladder just inside the door. A corn bin took up half the loft. Eaves of the roof came down to the floor. One small window gave a dim light.

"Here's where we sleep," Will said as he showed George a lumpy cornhusk mattress against the brick chimney. "There's a peg for your clothes and one for the drum. Now let's go down."

The big room below had a short wide bed built into one corner. People used to sleep half sitting up against large pillows. A chest held clothing and extra bedding. George heard a baby cry and saw the cradle near the hearth.

Mistress Spencer handed the baby to her

husband, who sat in the only chair, facing the fire. Strings of wrinkled red peppers, rings of dried pumpkin, and feathery bunches of herbs hung from the ceiling. Kegs of cornmeal and dried beans stood at one side of the fireplace. Above it hung Mr. Spencer's gun.

Mistress Spencer stirred a stew that bubbled in a black iron kettle hanging over the fire.

Will brought out two sawhorses, and George helped him lay the table board across them. They placed a bench on each side of the table. Will took two wooden plates, called trenchers, from the sideboard and held them for his mother to fill.

On the table were four spoons. George and Will ate from one trencher; Mr. and Mrs. Spencer shared the other. The stew was made of cornmeal, tiny wild onions, and oysters so big they had to be cut in three pieces to be swallowed. The boys drank fresh milk from wooden mugs.

After dinner the whir of Mrs. Spencer's spinning wheel made George drowsy. He and Will were soon asleep in the loft on the corn-husk mattress.

Before daylight of the next morning, George and his new family were up doing chores. The cow was milked and led up the riverbank to join the herd which shared James Citty's common pasture.

Water was brought from the nearest well, and clean sand for the floor was brought from the beach. Wood was split and stacked by the hearth. Eggs were hunted where half-wild chickens had made nests.

At about eight o'clock Mistress Spencer said it was time for school. With a gourd dipper she scooped water from a wooden bucket into a pewter washbasin. The boys washed their hands and faces, slicked down their hair, and set out.

School was held in the home of the Reverend Richard Buck. A dozen children came, including the Indian boy whom George had seen the day before. Only three were girls.

The Reverend Mr. Buck opened school with a prayer. Lessons were said aloud in a sing-song chorus. The Bible was the "reader."

For beginners, the minister had a "hornbook." It was a flat piece of wood about six inches long and four inches wide, with a stubby handle. The alphabet was printed on it in small and capital letters. Below the alphabet were syllables: ab, eb, ib, ob, ub. At the bottom was The Lord's Prayer. The wood was covered with a sheet of transparent yellowish horn, which gave the hornbook its name.

When a girl could read from the Bible and write her own name, her schooling ended. Boys were sometimes taught more writing and also "ciphering," or arithmetic. Children who misbehaved got a dose of "switch-tea."

George liked the young Indian, whose Christian name was Jonathan. After school ended at noon, they walked partway home together. Will had to cut a bundle of rushes from the marsh. His mother needed them for scouring. Jonathan caught a big terrapin and gave it to George. "Makes good soup," he said.

That afternoon Mr. Spencer took both boys to the woods to dig sassafras tree roots. The bark of these roots was shipped to England and made into medicine. It brought more money than any Virginia product except tobacco. Tobacco was the most important crop grown on Mr. Spencer's land.

Mr. Spencer sold tobacco and sassafras to pay for the passage of people who wanted to come from England to Virginia. For each person whose fare he paid, the Company would give him another 50 acres of land. The new

✠ A a b c d e f g h i j k l m n o p q
r ſ s t u v w x y z & a e i o u
A B C D E F G H I J K L M N O P Q
R S T U V W X Y Z.

a e i o u | a e i o u
ab eb ib ob ub | ba be bi bo bu
ac ec ic oc uc | ca ce ci co cu
ad ed id od ud | da de di do du

In the Name of the Father, & of the
Son, & of the Holy Ghoſt. *Amen.*

OUR Father, which art in
Heaven, hallowed be thy
Name, thy Kingdom come, thy
Will be done on Earth, as it is in
Heaven. Give us this Day our
daily Bread, and forgive us our
Treſpaſſes, as we forgive them
that Treſpaſs againſt us : And
lead us not into Temptation, but
deliver us from Evil. *Amen.*

James Citty children learned the
alphabet and the Lord's Prayer
from hornbooks like this one.

settler agreed to work for Mr. Spencer not less than four years to repay his passage. Then the worker would be free to claim land of his own.

That night the whole family sat by the fire peeling and cutting up sassafras roots. On other nights George and Will shelled corn. George scraped the dried ears against the edge of a spade held between his knees. The kernels drummed into a wooden pail in his lap.

Mistress Spencer's knitting needles would click as she made socks. Her husband would be whittling some wooden buttons for her. Often he would tell stories about Captain John Smith and about Pocahontas, the friendly Indian princess who brought meat and corn to James Fort when the first settlers were starving.

Will sometimes built a corncob tower for his baby sister, who was already crawling. Her mother had sewed broad straps, called "hanging sleeves," to the shoulders of the baby's dress. They held her up and guided her while she learned to walk.

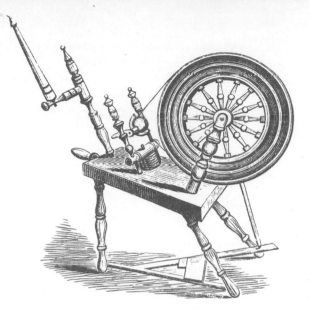

4. English Ways and Indian Ways

Since Mistress Spencer's only daughter was too young for housework, the boys helped with many kinds of tasks.

They learned to sand the floor smoothly, to make a twig broom, to shovel out the ashes while carefully guarding the fire, to clean the pig sty and the cowshed.

When Mistress Spencer had enough cream, they helped her make butter. She poured the cream into her small wooden churn. The round cover of the churn had a hole in its center for the dasher to pass through. The dasher was a long rod with a flat wooden cross nailed to the lower end. Will and George worked the dasher up and down.

At first the cream seemed to swell. Then golden specks of butter appeared. At last the butter clung to the dasher in a big yellow lump.

Mistress Spencer poured off the liquid, called buttermilk, washed the butter, and worked salt into it. Packed in wooden molds, it was stored in the cold loft for a rare treat.

One day the boys helped to make candles. During the fall, Will and his mother had gathered thousands of tiny wild bayberries and boiled them to get out the wax. Fifteen quarts of berries would make one pound of wax. Now Mistress Spencer put the gray-green mass of wax in a big kettle of warm water. It melted and floated on top.

Will got out the candle rods, each about three feet long with five notches evenly spaced near the center. His mother had already spun thick linen string for wicks. She tied a candle-length piece of string in every notch. Holding a rod level, she dipped the wicks into the melted wax.

Will had set the two trestles close together near the door, where it was cold. As each rod was dipped, it was hung across the trestles until the wax hardened. George helped, for the rods were so light he could use even his weak hand.

After about 25 dippings, shapely gray-green candles hung from every rod. They would burn with a clear light and give off the faint sweet bayberry fragrance.

The boys were also taught to save every feather when a chicken was cooked, or a wild duck, goose, or turkey was killed. A turkey wing became a hearth brush. Goose quills were made into writing pens. All other feathers went into pillows and mattresses. The Spencers hoped to have a "feather bed" some day.

Whenever Mrs. Spencer needed a supply of straight pins, she would send the boys to find a honey-locust tree. The long tough locust thorns made the best pins she could get for her sewing projects.

The making of clothes was the biggest job of the colonial housewife. For woolens, she began with sheared sheep wool from which she cut out matted knots and burrs. The wool was then washed, dyed, and carded. Cards were wooden paddles set with hooked wire teeth. A handful of wool was put between two cards

Line and Hemp,
being rated in water,
and dried again, 1.
are braked with a
wooden Brake, 2.
where the Shives 3.
fall down, then they
are heckled with an
Iron Heckle, 4.
where the Tow 5.
is parted from it.
    Flax is tied to
a Distaff, 6.
by the Spinster, 7.
which with her left
hand pulleth out
the Thred, 8.
and with her right
hand turneth a Wheel 9.
or a Spindle, 10.
upon which is
a Wharl. 11.
    The Spool receiveth
the Thred, 13.
which is drawn thence
upon a Yarn-windle; 14.
hence either Clewes 15.
are wound up,
or Hanks, 16
are made.

This old drawing shows the steps used to make linen
thread in James Citty in the seventeenth century.

and the teeth were pulled through it. After the wool was combed into strands and fluffed, it was ready for spinning.

Spinning meant twisting several strands of wool into one strong strand of thread or yarn. A fast-turning spindle did the twisting. The big spinning wheel turned the spindle. A spinner stood up to operate the wool wheel. She wound the ends of several strands onto the spindle. Her left hand held a bunch of wool just the right distance from it. Her right held a short rod, called a driver, with which she turned the wheel.

The spinning wheel hummed with a sound like wind. The spinner stepped back three steps, holding the yarn as it twisted and quivered. Suddenly she glided forward and let the yarn wind on the spindle. A good spinner walked 20 miles a day to make six skeins.

It took four days of spinning to make enough yarn for one day of weaving on a loom. This weaving produced three yards of broadcloth.

For summer clothes or underwear, the housewife converted flax plants into linen thread. Cloth woven from both linen thread and wool yarn was called "linsey-woolsey."

No wonder cloth and clothing were among

the most popular items brought by English merchant ships to the settlements along the river. Colonists traded sassafras, soap ashes, tobacco, and furs for cloth, tools, cooking utensils, and other things they needed.

The settlers got their best furs from the Indians. One mild February morning Mr. Spencer took the boys with him when he and his neighbors went upriver in a borrowed boat to trade for furs. They sailed with the rising tide, west along the James then north up the Chickahominy River to the Indian village.

A round palisade of poles ten feet high encircled the town. Its narrow entrance was designed like the opening of a snail shell. The Indians helped Mr. Spencer and his friends carry their trade goods into the town. About twenty houses stood close to the palisade, facing an open area.

George followed Mr. Spencer into a one-room house. It was as warm as an oven and smoky. The fire pit was in the center of the dirt floor; a smoke hole was in the roof above it.

Knee-high sleeping benches covered with rush mats stood against two walls. Furs were piled there for bedding. Baskets of shelled corn were stacked at one end of the room.

This picture of a Virginia Indian village, painted in 1585, includes the Indians' mat-covered houses; some tobacco and corn fields; and groups of Indians praying, eating, dancing, and hunting.

An Indian man and woman sharing some food

Indian women wove the rush mats, which formed the house walls and covered the benches. They wove baskets of many sizes, too.

Men did the hunting and cleared the fields, while the women and children did the planting and harvesting.

Indian mothers fed their families much the same foods as did the mothers of James Citty: corn, beans, pumpkins and squash, deer meat, turkey, terrapins, and seafood. Women pounded corn into meal and dried meat for future use.

The Indians had no cattle to tend. In place of milk they sometimes made *pohickora* of

40

pounded hickory nuts, walnuts, and acorns, shell and all, mixed with water. The shell fragments would sink, and the thick, white, oily "milk" was skimmed off and eaten on cornbread, hot from the fire. Settlers reported that it tasted rather like cream.

Making clothes was a long hard job for the Indian women, too. They spent weeks curing deerskins. Then the skins were cut, fringed, and sewed with bone needles.

During much of the year, children under the age of ten did not wear any clothing. Their mothers coated them with a thick salve blended

The Indian method of broiling fish. The picture on this page and opposite were painted in 1585 by John White, a settler in the ill-fated Roanoke colony.

The broyling of their fish ouer the flame of fier.

from bloodroot juice and melted bear grease. The salve reddened their tawny skin but kept it supple and protected it from heat, cold, and mosquito bites.

Older children and grownups wore skirts and cloaks or breech cloths and leggings, all made of deerskin. Some were beautifully beaded; a chief's cloak was a work of art. It might be softest leather embroidered with tiny seashells or made entirely of colorful turkey feathers.

While Mr. Spencer and his neighbors were busy trading, George and Will watched some boys play Indian soccer. They could use only their feet to move the ball toward the goal posts. The ball was made of deerskin stuffed with hair or moss. Players were quick and agile. "They make their goals as we do, only they never fight or pull one another down," George later told Mr. Spencer.

The day's trading had gone very well. Mr. Spencer even had a cornhusk doll to give his little girl. The Indians feasted their guests on smoked oysters, terrapin roasted in the shell, squirrel stew, and corn bread.

George and Will curled up in the bottom of the boat among the furs and slept most of the way home to James Citty.

42

5. T-i-m-b-e-r!

George was amazed that everyone in James
Citty kept a big fire going all day. In England
firewood was so scarce and expensive that only
wealthy people could afford all the heat they
wanted. He was surprised, too, by the amount
and the variety of forest products the colonists
shipped to their mother country.

Virginia was a woodsman's paradise. In their
journals, the settlers noted "fourteen sorts of
sweet-smelling timber trees. The highest and
reddest cedars in the world" grew in Virginia,
they wrote. The great oaks could be trimmed

to timbers two and one-half feet square and sixty feet long.

The dense shade of such forest giants killed undergrowth. In some groves there was space to drive a four-horse coach between the trees.

Other forests stood in swampland and grew thick as a jungle. Vines entangled the trees, while briars matted the undergrowth. Shrouds of morning fog added a touch of mystery.

One February day George went to the woods with Will and Mr. Spencer where they saw a small tree on which some apricot-pink fruit remained. Eating the dried fruit was a furry gray animal "about the bigness of a cat, with a head like a pig and a tail like a rat."

"Opposum!" Will pointed. "He's up that persimmon tree. A 'possum is good to eat, George. So are persimmons."

"When they're full ripe, persimmons are delicious," said Mr. Spencer. "But never taste one before the frost. Then they're so harsh and chokey they draw a man's mouth awry."

Later they heard the ringing sound of an ax and came upon a farmer clearing land. Cutting down the large trees was difficult for a man alone. This farmer was killing trees by chopping a broad ring of bark from around the trunk. Next he would trim off the small branches to let in sunlight. Afterward he would plant tobacco or corn and beans between the trees. Land that had been forest floor for centuries produced splendid crops.

In another part of the forest, they found men cutting trees for lumber. A great pine toppled toward the cutters.

"'Ware t-i-m-b-e-r!" shouted the foreman. And America's early lumberjacks jumped clear as the giant crashed.

Trunks and large limbs were hauled by oxcart to the lumberyard and cut to desired lengths by two men with a crosscut saw. Next an axman chopped off the rounded sides of each log to make a squared timber. The bark slabs would make roof shingles.

One woodcutter sharpened his ax on the whirling grindstone. Out flew a spray of golden sparks that delighted George and Will.

At the sawpit the boys watched two sawyers making planks. A squared timber was laid across the deep pit. One man stood on the broad timber and pulled the saw up. His partner stood in the pit and pulled the saw down, working in a shower of sawdust that sometimes made him sneeze.

Thin slats of hickory went to the cooper,
who made barrels. Oak, cedar, and pine were
cut up into clapboards for the housebuilders.
Boards of walnut and wild cherry, cedar and
oak were stacked for the furniture makers.
Much of the timber was shipped to England.

George and Will went on to the Pitch and
Tar Swamp where tar, charcoal, and potash
were being made.

The tar makers dug a hollow in the ground,
and above it they built a big cone of pine
logs. They heaped earth over the cone and set
a fire inside. As the pine logs burned, tar ran
down into the hollow. It was ladled into barrels

and sent to England's shipyards to seal the seams of her wooden vessels. A friendly workman gave each boy a lump of amber resin to chew.

The charcoalmakers stacked short lengths of oak and willow around a vent like a chimney. They covered the wood with moist turf and set it afire. But most of the wood only charred, turning black as coal. Charcoal was lighter to handle than wood. As a fuel, it gave off twice as much heat. The English needed charcoal to smelt iron ore and to make gunpowder.

The Virginia Company had hired men from

Poland to teach the colonists to make high-grade potash. They burned poplar and elm, ash and hickory logs. Big hollow trees that were still alive produced the best ashes.

Men shoveled the ashes into wooden tubs with holes in the bottom. They were propped up on platforms. Boiling water poured over the ashes ran down into iron pots on the ground. This liquid was called lye. The lye was strained and boiled down. When cool, it formed a solid lump of potash ready for use in making soap or glass either in Jamestown or in England.

Before returning home, Mr. Spencer and the boys stopped at a farm on Back River, where two men were building a small boat for Mr. Spencer.

There were so few skilled boatbuilders in the colony that Mr. Spencer had tried to trade for an Indian canoe to avoid waiting. "But they wanted my ax or Mrs. Spencer's kettle," he said. "And we can't spare those. The Indians don't like to trade their boats. Shaping a canoe out of a tree trunk is a long, hard job."

"How can they do it without axes?" George asked.

"They fell a large white pine by burning

Virginia Indians making a dugout canoe

through its base," Mr. Spencer said. "Then they build fires along the log and scrape out the charred wood with sharp stones or shells. They burn and scrape until they hollow the log. They shape the bow and stern with their shells or stone hatchets."

"How big a boat can they make?" asked George.

"Indian canoes are from 20 to 40 feet long and about 45 inches deep," Mr. Spencer told him. "They're sturdy and swift. Any settler who gets one is lucky. Since the river is our main highway, every family needs a boat."

6. Corn, Tobacco, and Silk

The Virginia forest in April was a green lace of new leaves starred with white dogwood blossoms. Wildflowers made the air smell sweet. But the settlers had scant time to enjoy such beauty.

Spring was their busiest season. Every man, no matter what his regular work, must also plant his corn, flax, and tobacco. All hands were needed, so school was let out.

The English settlers planted as the Indians had taught them. George, his arm nearly healed, helped the Spencers. In wide holes about a yard apart, they set four grains of corn and two or three beans close enough for the bean vines to climb the corn stalks. If fertilizer were needed, they would bury a few fish under the seed. When the corn was knee-high, they would hoe a little hill of earth around the stalk. In the three-foot spaces between the hills, they grew pumpkin vines.

Like the Indians, they raised three kinds of corn—popcorn, hominy or flint corn, and dent, or meal corn. Seed planted in April, May, and June, became "roasting ears" in late July, August, and September.

In early spring tiny tobacco seeds mixed with ashes were sown in sheltered plots. The seedbeds were covered with oak leaves and branches until the frosts were gone. By early May when the uncovered seedlings had sprouted four leaves, they were ready to set out, wide apart, in fields and forest clearings.

Meanwhile the fish were running upriver. Young sturgeon a yard long, great shoals of herring, big shad, rockfish, perch, and bass all seemed to come at once. Later, George was amazed to see sturgeon, six to eight feet long.

The Indians had taught the settlers to spear large fish and build traps of stakes and brushwood to catch the smaller ones. Since nets

and boats were scarce, several men would fish together. They fastened one end of a long net on shore. Two men in a skiff would tow the big net into the river, enclosing as large an area as possible. They brought the other end ashore. Later everyone would help to haul it in, loaded with fish.

Most of the catch had to be salted for winter. George split and cleaned fish, salting layer after layer as it was packed in a barrel.

By the time the barrel was full, he was sick of fish!

Everyone worked from dawn to dusk. Not until the stars came out did George have time to practice his drumming. Sometimes a chorus of frogs joined in. And mockingbirds sang all night when the moon was full.

Out of the grass on dark evenings rose fire-flies—a wonder George had never seen. There were hundreds of golden sparkles flying in the air. Other insects whined about his ears and bit him.

"Mosquitoes," said Will. "You just have to get used to them."

Will showed George how to get honey from honeysuckle, where to find wild strawberries, shiny blackberries, and fat blueberries, as each fruit ripened. The perfume of wild grapes in bloom drifted through the woods, promising juicy mouthfuls of purple fruit by late summer.

Mr. Spencer decided it was time to notify Governor Yeardley that George's arm was as good as new. He might be expected to join his former shipmates, now settled at Berkeley.

George and Mr. Spencer found the Governor near the river, inspecting the town's first guesthouse.

"At present there is no boat going out to Berkeley, George," the Governor said. "But James Citty needs a drummer boy. Would you like to stay here?"

"Very much, sir!" George meant it.

"Good. Report to me on Monday next."

"Yes, sir. Thank you, sir." George remembered to salute.

On their way home Mr. Spencer and George visited the Governor's new silkworm house. The long narrow building was set in a grove of wild mulberry trees, for mulberry leaves are the only food silkworms will eat.

Silk was in great demand in England. The colonists were urged to produce silk. Mr. Spencer wanted to learn more about it.

"We brought silkworm eggs on the *Supply*," George boasted.

The keeper overheard him. "Our worms hatched from those very eggs," he said.

The building had an odd-looking chimney with no inside fireplace. The fireplace was outdoors because smoke injured the worms; heat entered through holes the size of flowerpots.

Fishnets hung over the open windows to keep out the birds. Down the center of the room ran tiers of eighteen-inch cubicles. In the cubicles thousands of slender ash-gray worms chewed busily on mulberry leaves. George heard their steady *sh-sh-sh*.

When full-grown to about three inches, they would stop eating and climb up twigs that had been placed in the cubicles. Within three days each worm would spin itself inside a cocoon, or envelope, of 800 to 1,200 yards of fine silk strands.

Women would steam the cocoons over boiling water and unreel the silk. Five or six strands twisted together would make a thread strong enough for weaving into cloth.

Silk making took only two months, but they were the busiest months of spring. The Company had offered the settlers a bonus to produce silk: 50 pounds of tobacco for a single pound of wound silk. Even so, Mr. Spencer decided that growing tobacco suited him better than the delicate silkworm business.

Once a week the settlers had to get the weeds and worms out of their tobacco. This was hard, hot work, but tobacco was money. Many farmers had neglected their food crops to grow tobacco, so now even corn was scarce. As a result, the Assembly passed a law that only 100 pounds of first quailty tobacco per person could be brought to market this year.

By mid-July each tall plant was topped by a spray of pink flowers. The Spencers pinched these off so the leaves would grow larger. Next, sprouts called suckers appeared between leaf and stalk and at the top of the plant. These must be pinched off too. They took food from the all-important leaves.

Tobacco ripened in late August. The choice leaves would be picked and strung on cord lines to dry, slowly turning from green to golden brown. Then the cord was removed and the golden leaves were twisted into thick ropes or rolled into balls.

Packed in barrels, the tobacco was taken by boat or oxcart to a public warehouse. There Company inspectors examined and weighed it. Any tobacco not properly dried was "burnt before the owner's face," according to law.

The inspector gave each grower a receipt for the amount he accepted. Anything could be bought, and fines or taxes could be paid with these tobacco receipts.

But George could not help Mr. Spencer harvest his crop. By harvest time he was living in the servants' quarters of the Governor's house, as James Citty's new drummer boy.

An old print shows tobacco leaves hanging up to dry; being rolled and stacked in barrels; inspected and weighed at the storehouse.

7. Happenings in the Church

Now George had to practice regularly on his drum. Governor Yeardley, a military man, expected him to beat "reveille" at daylight to wake the town and summon guardsmen to their duties. He beat "tattoo" at night to warn townsfolk to be at home, to summon guardsmen back to their quarters, and to post sentries.

When there was news, he drummed for the town crier. Standing on a platform in the marketplace, he would beat "assembly" until a crowd gathered to listen. And he drummed for the bodyguards to drill in Blockhouse Field near the isthmus.

On Sundays George's rolling drum called all the people of the area to church. They came by boat from up, down, and across the river. They trooped from the mainland over the isthmus.

Everyone belonged to the same church. Before boarding ship for Virginia, the colonists had pledged loyalty to the Church of England. Everyone not sick abed was expected at Sunday services.

In winter some people brought small metal foot stoves for warmth in the unheated building. Those living at a distance brought their lunch. The service might last three hours, followed by Sunday School in the afternoon.

The settlers, many of whom could not read, enjoyed hearing the Bible recited from the King James Version. Most liked to come, if only because it was the one time during the week when they could get together. Before and after the services they gossiped with old friends and met new arrivals.

Most of the social life of the early colonists centered in the church. Christmas, then celebrated on January 6th, was a happy time. At weddings and baptisms there was feasting, singing, and folk dancing. Just for fun, the

men would fire off their guns. Even a funeral was a time of family reunion.

James Citty folk might have to walk to church through dust or mud, but they wore their best clothes. The styles were the same they had known in England, but some were better dressed in America than they had been at home.

"Here our cow keeper on Sundays goes dressed in fresh flaming silk," wrote the Colony's secretary. "And the wife of one who in England was a poor coal miner, wears her beaver hat with a fair pearl hatband and a silken suit."

The children looked like miniature adults. Boys wore long-sleeved shirts, knee breeches, waistcoats, or vests and, in cold weather, suit coats. Their hand-knit stockings were tied up with string, and their buckled shoes fit either foot, or neither.

Girls wore long petticoats, long-sleeved blouses, and long skirts. Over the blouse went a laced bodice and over the skirt an apron. In winter they wore hooded cloaks. Girls' shoes might have rosettes instead of buckles, but they fit no better.

Cotton cloth, imported from India, was almost unknown to the colonists. Their coolest clothes were too hot for comfort in Virginia's sticky summer weather.

Summer was the dreaded "sickly season." One steamy August afternoon, George became ill in church. His teeth chattered from a sudden chill, and he ached in every bone. Then the chill changed to a burning fever.

The Governor's housekeeper took him home and put him to bed.

"It's the 'seasoning,'" she told the Governor. "If he lives, he will never have it again." And she nursed George back to health.

The Yeardleys were preparing to turn over the house to the new governor, Sir Francis Wyatt. In mid-October, the James Citty cannon fired a salute to an incoming ship. George was well enough to drum for Governor Yeardley and his honor guard as they marched to the dock to receive Sir Francis. George was kept busy, for six shiploads of settlers came with Wyatt, and each group received an official welcome.

In November Governor Wyatt was inaugurated, and the Virginia Assembly met. George was the drummer for the ceremonies, all of which took place in church.

The members of the First Assembly were elected by the settlements and met in James Citty in 1619 to make laws for the colony of Virginia.

It was in the same small church, two years earlier, that representative government began in the New World. On July 30, 1619, Governor Yeardley had called together the members of his Council and 22 burgesses, or representatives. Two burgesses had been elected from each of the colony's eleven settlements. They met to "establish one equal and uniform government over all Virginia."

Governor Yeardley and his honor guard had led the solemn procession to church that day. Next walked members of the Council, wearing big beaver hats. Swords clanked at their sides. The burgesses followed.

The Reverend Richard Buck had opened the meeting with prayer. Then each burgess took the oath of allegiance to King James. The Governor read his orders from the Virginia Company, urging the colonists to produce iron, silk, and wine for export.

The Virginia lawmakers had sat with their hats on, as did the members of Parliament in England. When a man wanted to speak, he removed his hat, stood up, and waited for the Governor to call on him. Perspiring in the midsummer heat, swatting flies and mosquitoes, they worked earnestly to make fair laws for Virginia.

Some of the laws regulated farming. Some punished men for gambling, getting drunk, or refusing to work. One law taxed a man according to the cost of the clothes he and his wife wore to church on Sunday!

Other 1619 laws dealt with conduct toward the Indians. Any colonist who traded guns or ammunition to the Indians would be hanged as a traitor. Anyone who gave or sold them "an English dog of quality—mastiff, bloodhound, greyhound, spaniel, or any other—" could be fined almost two days' wages.

Every settlement was urged "to obtain by just means" a few Indian "boyes of witt and grace" to be taught "true religion" and fitted for the college that was to be built for them.

That First Assembly also had sat as a court. One colonist was punished for taking an Indian's canoe; and another, for forcing some Indians to sell him corn at gunpoint. "Such outrages could breed danger and loss of life to others," warned the lawmakers. They ordered all settlers to do nothing "that might disturb the present peace" with the Indians.

In the intense heat that August of 1619, several burgesses fell ill and one died. But they had made history. They ended by reminding the Virginia Company of London that it had promised them a voice in their own government.

The members of the First Assembly in 1619 had planted the seed of colonial independence.

8. Journey up the James

On a brisk November morning soon after the close of the 1621 Assembly, Governor Wyatt's shallop, a small craft with sail and oars, moved upriver on the rising tide.

The new treasurer of the colony, Mr. George Sandys, was in command. Since he represented the Governor, four of the honor guards and the drummer went with him. Young George was looking forward to seeing his old friends at Berkeley, where they were to spend a night.

Treasurer Sandys not only carried the new Governor's greetings to the settlers, but he also encouraged them to produce more things to sell in England, where stockholders were demanding returns on their investment in the Virginia Company. He was taking a new manager to the ironworks at Falling Creek, 66 miles upriver.

The smelting of iron had begun there two years earlier but stopped when the manager and his foreman had died.

The journey must be swift, for the river might soon freeze and trap the travelers.

Their first stop was at Southampton, a busy settlement where the Chickahominy flowed into the James. The Indian town that George had visited with Mr. Spencer was near here. A number of Indian children seemed to be living happily with the settlers.

Leaving Southampton, the shallop called at two smaller settlements, one ten and one twenty miles away. The new manager of the ironworks looked worried. "Our people live so far apart, how can they help each other if the savages attack?" he asked.

"The Company wants settlers planted ten miles apart, so the plantations will have room to grow," Mr. Sandys explained. "They believe the Indians will now remain peaceful."

At Berkeley, George drummed for the Treasurer and his honor guards to land. They were welcomed by people George had known on the *Supply*. Chaplain Pawlet greeted him warmly. But of the Tracys, he saw only Tom.

Mr. and Mrs. Tracy were dead. Sadly Tom showed George their sturdy house, new vines, and mulberry trees. His sister had married and moved to her husband's place across the river. Tom was so lonely he talked of going back to England on the first ship.

Berkeley stood on land between James River and a creek. A high log palisade from river to creek fenced in 400 acres. Tom, who had helped build the fence, bragged that it was "horse-high, bull-proof, and pig-tight." Before it was built, many farm animals had strayed off or been killed by the Indians.

For dinner the visitors enjoyed a treat—wild goose and roast pork with English vegetables. The carrots, cabbage, and turnips had grown from seed the Tracys brought.

"Stay with us longer," Chaplain Pawlet urged Mr. Sandys the next morning. "Each year we celebrate November 30, the date on which the first Berkeley settlers reached Virginia. It is our holy day of Thanksgiving."

But the travelers dared not stay, for already ice was forming in the marshes.

As they sailed on upstream, Mr. Sandys showed George a map of Virginia. The colony was divided into four "corporations": Elizabeth Citty on Hampton Roads at the river's mouth, James Citty, Charles Citty, and Henrico, farthest up the James to the west. "We're in Charles Citty Corporation now," he said.

The town itself was the next stop. Charles Citty stood on steep clay cliffs where the Appomattox River enters the James from the south. A palisade two miles long, built from river to river, fortified the site. Here cattle, goats, sheep, pigs, and horses could feed in safety. No other settlement had so many animals.

A free school for English and Indian children was soon to open at Charles Citty. After finishing this school, Indian boys could enter the college which was being started by the English farther upriver. The travelers expected to reach the College Lands by nightfall.

From Charles Citty the shallop had to be rowed for many of the fourteen winding miles called the "Curls" of the James. Hour after hour, eight heavy oars creaked and splashed.

The voyagers passed Henrico, once intended for the capital but now almost deserted. About two miles farther north, cold and weary, they landed at the main settlement on the College Lands. They were warmly welcomed by the manager, Mr. George Thorpe. Some of his farm families gave them lodging.

The College Lands stretched for ten miles along the north river bank. Ten thousand acres had been set aside by the Virginia Company to build the college and provide farms to support it. Money for the college was given by English church members who had been charmed by the Christian Indian princess, Pocahontas, when she visited London in 1616. They believed that some Christian Indians, trained as farmers and craftsmen, would help in the peaceful settling of Virginia.

The English did not know then that most Indian parents would refuse to send their children to a white man's school. To the Indians, their forest lore was far more useful than an English education. Many suspected that the settlers really meant to hold their sons as hostages or enslave them.

Mr. Thorpe believed that time and kind treatment would change the Indians' minds. He was

Pocahontas became the wife of John Rolfe, one of the earliest settlers in James Citty. She was remembered in later years for her aid to the struggling new town.

trying hard to convert Chief Opechancanough. To win him over, Mr. Thorpe had "a faire English house" built especially for him. Opechancanough reacted like a child with a new toy. The house key so fascinated him that he would lock and unlock his door a hundred times a day.

All Indians were welcome at the College Lands. When one was attacked and torn by English mastiffs, Mr. Thorpe had the valuable watchdogs shot. Some of his tenants complained that the manager was becoming too friendly for his own safety and theirs.

Mr. Sandys looked worried when he saw Mr. Thorpe lend his musket to an Indian warrior so he could hunt deer. During the busy season many of his farmers did the same, Mr. Thorpe said. It was quite safe. Letting their Indian brothers do all the hunting gave the settlers time for more important work. The 1619 law forbidding such action had quietly fallen into disuse.

Next day the Sandys party left for their final stop, the ironworks. As they rowed northward snow began to fall. George was awed by the majesty of the silent, snow-draped forest.

The shallop turned into Falling Creek. At the ironworkers' village the travelers waded ashore through a mush of ice, but the settlers

These tools, unearthed at the site of James Citty, may have been forged from iron made in Virginia.

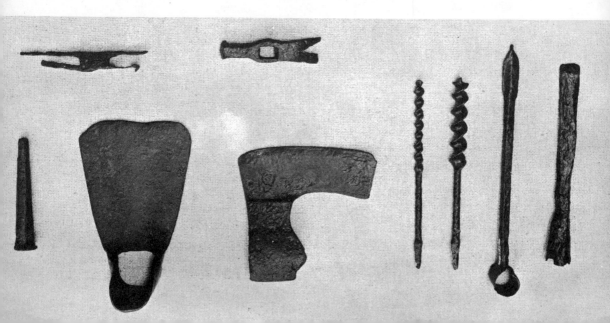

welcomed them with roaring fires and hot food.

The new manager thought the place ideal. It had forests of fuel, plenty of water, large boulders in the creekbed to supply needed limestone, and a rich vein of ore.

His son and twenty skilled workmen had come to the site a month earlier. Some of the original ironworkers still lived here. Together they were repairing the furnace and forge. The new manager promised that within three months they would be in production.

Well pleased, Mr. Sandys gave orders for the long return trip. Where the river narrowed, ice reached out from shore like silent fingers threatening to choke the channel. The rowers wrapped their hands in rags and kept doggedly on. They had to win this race with winter. On the last day they used both sails and oars to force the shallop through the ice film that covered the James.

When they arrived at the capital, Mr. Sandys reported to Governor Wyatt. He did not seem impressed by the peace that apparently prevailed. "The Company would be wise," said Mr. Sandys, "to grant our Assembly's petition that 'plantations' draw closer together in these doubtful times between us and the Indians."

9. First Factories in Virginia

After the wintry trip upriver, George was glad to be warm in the Governor's house. Called the Country House, it was then the best-built and largest home in James Citty. The first story was of brick, and under the eastern half was a brick-paved cellar.

In the Great Hall the Governor's armchair stood at the head of a long table. At important dinners a silver salt-and-spice holder graced the center of the table. Guests sat on chairs and benches. They ate from pewter plates with pewter spoons and knives. Napkins a yard square were tied around their necks.

The house had casement windows with small panes of greenish glass set in lead. Candles in sticks and wall brackets lighted the rooms.

The downstairs ceilings were plastered with white oystershell lime. Choice wood was used for paneled walls. The Great Hall even had the luxury of a carpet.

The family bedroom and guest room were upstairs. The Governor's fourposter bed had a deep feather mattress and curtains that could be closed to keep out the cold. Near it a washstand held a wide bowl and pitcher of water. After washing or shaving, the Governor poured the used water into a slop jar which a servant would empty.

The Governor's looking glass stood on the clothes chest. His suits hung in a wardrobe, a tall and spacious piece of furniture nearly as big as a closet.

Sometimes George waited in the office while Governor Wyatt wrote a message for him to deliver. The Governor's sharpened goose-quill pen would dip deep into the inkhorn and scratch across the paper. He would shake fine sand over the ink to blot it. Then he would fold and seal the note with a blob of wax melted over the flame of his candle.

George's duties as a drummer kept him from attending school. In his free time he watched the craftsmen whose apprentices he knew. He especially liked to watch the potter.

The potter's wheel was a revolving flat disk set in a small table. He spun the top disk by kicking a connecting wheel at floor level. After he had centered a ball of clay on the spinning top disk, the potter pressed his thumbs into the heart of the clay ball until it opened like a bowl. At his sure touch, the sides of the bowl flared outward or rose higher. The clay seemed alive in his hands. When the bowl suited the potter, he cut it off the wheel by sliding a piece of taut string under the base. His apprentice carried it outside to dry.

Sun-dried clay bowls, plates, pitchers, and mugs were sprinkled with powdered lead. Then they were baked in a kiln, or oven. The heat made them shiny, hard, and waterproof.

Clay bricks were fired in a different type of kiln. George watched an Indian, who sometimes helped the brickmaker, place several clay pipes in the brick kiln. The Indian's brown clay pipes were popular in James Citty. They smoked well, and they were tax free. A tax made English white clay pipes expensive.

This potter's wheel is spun by a belt connected to another wheel, instead of by a kick wheel.

"A man grows his own tobacco, and King James taxes him for a pipe to smoke it in," the colonists complained.

Once when Treasurer Sandys had business at the new Glasshouse across the isthmus, he took George along. Six glassmakers had been brought from Venice to make items the settlers needed—bottles, window glass, and colored beads for trade with the Indians. They had restored furnaces built in 1608 by Polish glassmakers. Now they were making some "trialls," or samples.

George watched as the glassmaker thrust the flared end of an iron blow pipe into a bowl of red-hot melted glass inside the main furnace. When he withdrew the pipe, a glowing ball of soft glass stuck to it.

The glassmaker blew into the pipe's wooden mouthpiece, and the glowing ball of glass ballooned. He nodded to his apprentice, who touched the bottom of the golden balloon with an iron rod that he had dipped in molten glass. The balloon stuck to the rod, and the glassmaker twisted off the blowpipe.

A master workman took the rod and sat down on a backless chair with long iron arms.

The glassmaker blows into a long iron tube to form melted glass into the correct size and shape.

He rolled the rod on the chair arms, shaping the balloon with a special tool that looked like flat-bladed shears. He worked fast, for the glass was cooling and beginning to turn green. George saw that he was shaping a bottle.

Finally, with a quick twist of the special tool, the master cracked the bottle off the rod and handed it to Mr. Sandys. It still had to be hardened in the annealing furnace, he told him, but first the Treasurer might like to show it to Governor Wyatt.

Carrying the precious bottle, George walked home across the isthmus beside Mr. Sandys. Back River was peppered with wild ducks and geese resting on their flight north. The wind that stirred the marsh grass promised an early spring.

George saw farmers preparing their fields for planting and heard the tapping of hammers on a new building. The colonists were looking forward to a time of peace and progress this first of March, 1622.

There was no hint of the horror just ahead.

10. Virginia Fights for Life

To the west, trouble was already brewing. It began with one of Chief Opechancanough's best warriors, called Jack-of-the-Feathers because of the fantastic way he decorated himself. One day Jack took an English trader named Morgan on a trading trip to the Indian village on the Pamunkey (York) River.

Three days later Jack returned wearing Morgan's cap. He said the trader was dead, but he would not tell what had happened. Morgan's two young servants tried to take the Indian to the Governor for questioning. He refused to go. As he stalked off, one of them shot and wounded him. They put him in a boat and set out for James Citty. But on the way Jack died.

When this news reached Opechancanough, he flew into a rage. He hated the English anyway. Their peace treaty meant nothing to him. He had only pretended friendship until he thought the time was right to strike.

Now he called his important men to a secret meeting. Too long the English had wronged his people, he said. Each year the huge white-winged canoes brought more white intruders. Each year they took more Indian land. Each year they felled more trees. They sent shiploads of trees across the ocean! In time they would destroy the forests—home of the animals that gave the Indians food and clothing.

"Our people will right these wrongs!" Opechancanough vowed. "Hear me and tell no white man what I say. Swear by the bones of our dead chiefs! I send this message to all my people.

"In thirteen nights comes the dark of the moon. On the fourteenth morning we strike down the white men.

"When the sun rises on that day, some of you appear at their homes as before, with meat or fish to trade. Others hide near their fields. At the appointed hour we strike at every house, sparing no one—man, woman, or child. Only when these spoilers are gone can we be safe in our dwelling places."

It happened that several days later Governor Wyatt sent some messengers and gifts to Opechancanough. As the new Governor, he sought to renew the peace treaty with the Indians. The Chief was most hospitable. He sent gifts to the Governor and a friendly reply. "I hold the peace so firm, the sky will fall before I dissolve it," declared Opechancanough.

The Indians seemed friendlier than ever as they waited for the dark of the moon.

Early on the morning of Good Friday, 1622, George was wakened by heavy pounding on the Governor's door. He ran and opened it. A settler from across James River stood there, pale and terrified.

"The Governor—I must see him at once!"

"It's the Indians, sir," cried the settler, as the Governor appeared. "When the sun is eight o'clock high they will attack every settlement up and down the James!"

"How do you know?"

"From my Indian boy, Chanco. I trust him

as I would my own son. Last night his Indian brother came to our place. Told him to murder me and my whole family this morning. But Chanco is loyal. He woke me at daylight and revealed the plot. I made my place secure and rowed across to warn you. When I landed near the blockhouse, I told Captain Powell."

Gunfire interrupted him. "The Captain's sent a runner to the mainland. The gun's to wake the town."

"Get your drum, boy!" the Governor told George. "March and bang for your life! Rouse the town crier! We must send messengers up and down the river." George sprang to obey.

May they be in time, he prayed. And how do we protect James Citty with our fort in ruins?

People from Glasshouse Point and farms on the mainland began to stream in, bringing their children, food, and weapons.

At eight o'clock sharp, the Indian "trading party" appeared on the isthmus. Greeted by a salvo of cannon from the blockhouse, they melted back into the woods. Soon more "traders" approached in canoes. Welcomed by musket fire, they also retreated.

James Citty folk spent a long tense day and

night watching for the Indians' return. George and the guardsmen slept on the wooden floor of the blockhouse between the cannon. But the long wicked whistling of Indian arrows was not heard at James Citty. Chanco's warning had saved the town.

Other settlements were not so lucky. Less than 10 miles downstream, 83 people were slain.

Southampton town defended itself, but five men working in the fields were killed. At former Governor Yeardley's farm six died. Across the river twenty more people were massacred.

From James Citty to the College Lands, settlers tried in vain to beat back the Indian attacks.

In some homes the Indians sat down to breakfast with their unsuspecting hosts. Then, seizing table knives or other handy tools, they slew them "most barbarously."

At Berkeley eleven settlers died. Tom Tracy had left for England, but across the James, his sister, her husband, and ten others were murdered. Their settlement was abandoned.

Charles Citty was hard hit. Twenty-seven people and whole herds of their animals were butchered. Henrico was burned to the ground. Five more men died there.

Up at the College Lands, Mr. Thorpe was busy with Easter plans when the warning came. He refused to believe that any Indian would harm him. So he died, with seventeen assistants who were working to open the Indian College.

At the ironworks, the most distant settlement, 27 men, women, and children perished. The furnace and forge were destroyed.

As survivors straggled into James Citty, the colony added up its losses. On March 22, 1622, 347 settlers had died. Countless homes had been burned, livestock killed, food supplies stolen or spoiled.

James Citty was severely overcrowded now.

People feared to return to lonely farms and settlements, so crops were not planted. Food became scarce. Disease flared and spread. Before the summer ended, more people died of illness and hunger than had been killed by the Indians.

The English were desperate. Since kindness had failed to win the savages, they reported to the Virginia Company, "We now have just cause to destroy them by all means possible." Former Governor Yeardley was made Marshal of Virginia. As soon as men could be properly armed, he led them to strike the Indian villages. The settlers were so brutal, they made enemies even of the few Indians who had not joined in the plot.

The only peaceful spot was Virginia's Eastern Shore, across Chesapeake Bay. There the English and the Indians had always dealt fairly with one another. Chief Debedeavon, "The Laughing King of Accomac," had refused to take part in the massacre.

Perhaps, said Sir George Yeardley, the Chief would allow some of the displaced settlers to live in Accomac, Indian name for the Eastern Shore. Governor Wyatt asked him to go there and see what could be done.

Seal of the Virginia Company

11. Beginnings of Greatness

Late in June Sir George Yeardley and several other leaders left James Citty aboard the colony's largest vessel, a 40-ton barque. They sought new settlements for people made homeless by the Indian attack.

To impress Chief Debedeavon they took bodyguards and the drummer. George was excited. Ahead lay the only part of the colony he had never seen.

They sailed down the James and eastward along Hampton Roads to Elizabeth Citty. The place had grown since the *Supply* had landed there nearly a year and a half earlier. George counted some 50 buildings on both sides of Hampton Creek.

The visitors stayed in two new guesthouses, shaded by magnolia trees the settlers called "the tulip-bearing laurel which has the pleasantest smell in the world." The head of the settlement proudly showed off his improvements—a brick-lined well, a silk house, and a wine press operated by Frenchmen.

Almost every house had its own palisade. No one had been killed here, but still the settlers feared to tend distant fields.

The guests had to be content to eat fish, crabs, and a little green corn grown near the forts. It was plain that very few refugees could be fed here at Elizabeth Citty.

The party sailed on to Virginia's Eastern Shore. After crossing Chesapeake Bay, the vessel anchored in King's Creek.

The travelers were welcomed by Thomas Savage who had come to Virginia as a boy in 1607. For three years he had lived in Chief Powhatan's village, learning the Indians' ways and language, and later had served the colony as interpreter. Then he had settled on the Eastern Shore, where Chief Debedeavon gave him land.

Now he arranged the meeting of Yeardley with Chief Debedeavon. George drummed for the ceremony that opened the conference. The parley was highly successful.

The Eastern Shore Indians were the easiest to deal with in Virginia. They were better farmers than those near James Citty, and they were honest traders. "By using little sticks, they keep as correct an account as the English," wrote one of the visitors.

Yeardley bought all the corn he could to feed the hungry at James Citty. He also secured the promise of new land for at least a hundred displaced settlers.

Before leaving, the Yeardley party visited the new saltworks. There, a maze of man-made channels brought sea water into shallow ponds to be evaporated by the sun's heat. In a saltern, or salt house, the job of obtaining salt crystals was finished by boiling.

This was the colonists' second attempt to make salt. It was badly needed, for only by salting could they preserve meat or fish for winter use. The new works had just been started, so the visitors could take only a little salt to James Citty.

After three weeks on the Eastern Shore, they

sailed back across the bay. Seeing former Governor Yeardley relaxed on deck, George perched near him on a coil of rope. Shyly he asked: "Sir, people say you may soon go home to England. Is that true?"

"England—home?" Sir George sounded startled. "Why, lad, I've lived in Virginia since 1610. When I first saw it, James Fort was a shambles. Most of the people had died in the 'starving time' the winter before. Of 500 settlers, only 60 had survived—and they were walking skeletons! Sir Thomas Gates, who was in charge, decided we must abandon Virginia. We went aboard ship and started home to England."

Now George was startled. "What happened, sir?"

"That day the colony was saved by a near-miracle," Yeardley answered. "Halfway down the James we met the advance guard of our first governor, Thomas, Lord De la Warr, sailing upstream. Lord De la Warr himself was already at Elizabeth Citty with three ship-loads of supplies and 150 new settlers to help rebuild the fort."

"Through all our struggles since then, we have come to love this place. Things are hard now, but next year who knows? We may be rich! This spring we received from the Indies some 'cotton-wool' plants which prosper exceedingly well here. And my potato vines from Bermuda are flourishing."

"That sounds fine, sir!"

"London Town is sending us a hundred new settlers with ample supplies and weapons from its arsenal in the Tower. Virginia has room for thousands more. An Indian chief once told me that over the high hills, far to the west, lies another great sea. One day perhaps, my children's children may know the true breadth of this land. No, my lad, not England, but Virginia is my dear home."

"Thank you, sir," George said happily. He knew that England was no longer home to him, either. He was glad to be going home to James Citty. It might be only a village in size, but it was in every way the capital of a bountiful new land. To George his new homeland promised a fine and challenging future!

For 92 years, James Fort, James Citty or James Towne was the capital of the ever-growing colony. Then, in 1699, after the fourth State House there had been destroyed by fire, the capital was moved to higher ground seven miles inland. First called Middle Plantation, this settlement was renamed Williamsburg, in honor of King William, who then ruled England.

Visitors today roam through the reconstructed James Fort on the mainland. Then they visit the marshy island where a ruined church tower and a few brick foundations still mark the site of America's first colonial capital.

Glossary

"assembly": a signal on a bugle or drum for people to gather to listen to the news

barque: a sailing ship which has three masts

blockhouse: a two-story fort made of heavy wood, with openings in the sides to shoot from

bloodroot juice: juice from a bloodroot plant which has a red root and red sap

broadcloth: a fine, smooth woolen cloth which was made in widths rather than yards

ciphering: figuring problems in arithmetic

cooper: a barrelmaker

crockery: pots, jars, dishes, etc., made of baked clay

dasher: a rotating device used in a churn for stirring cream

flax: a blue-flowered plant, the fibers of which may be spun into linen thread

flint corn: Indian corn having hard kernels that do not shrivel

forge: a place where metal is heated so that it can be formed into any shape

hominy: hulled and dried corn kernels, broken into hard bits and and boiled for food

kiln: an oven used for drying or baking bricks or pottery

looking glass: a mirror

millstones: circular stones between which grain is ground in a windmill

musket: a hand gun with a long barrel

palisade: a fence made of large, pointed stakes

parley: a meeting to discuss or settle something

pewter: a soft mixture of metals from which such utensils as mugs, spoons, and dishes were made

"reveille": a signal calling the guardsmen to duty in the morning

rosette: a ribbon formed in the shape of a rose

salvo: the firing of many guns or cannons, one after another or at the same time

skiff: a light rowboat

slop jar: the basin or bowl into which was poured the waste water from cleaning, etc.

spoilers: those who took land and territory by force

stove in: smashed in

"switch-tea": a beating or whipping with a switch

"tattoo": a signal on the drum or bugle, warning the people to be in their homes and guardsmen to be in their quarters

terrapin: a turtle whose flesh is used for food

whittling: carving by cutting thin shavings from the wood

Index